Lerner SPORTS

SPORTS
ALL-STARS

CHRIS PAUL

Jon M. Fishman

Lerner Publications ◆ Minneapolis

Lerner Publications Company
An imprint of Lerner Publishing Group, Inc.
241 First Avenue North
Minneapolis, MN 55401 USA

For reading levels and more information, look up this title at www.lernerbooks.com.

Main body text set in Albany Std. Typeface provided by Agfa.

Library of Congress Cataloging-in-Publication Data

Names: Fishman, Jon M., author.
Title: Chris Paul / Jon M. Fishman.
Description: Minneapolis : Lerner Publications, [2020] | Series: Sports all-Stars | Includes bibliographical references and index. | Audience: Ages 7–11 | Audience: Grades 4–6 | Summary: "Point guard Chris Paul not only led the NBA four times in assists and six times in steals-he also won two gold medals. Get to know this Houston Rockets hero!"— Provided by publisher.
Identifiers: LCCN 2019028770 (print) | LCCN 2019028771 (ebook) | ISBN 9781541577305 (library binding) | ISBN 9781541589520 (paperback) | ISBN 9781541583542 (ebook)
Subjects: LCSH: Paul, Chris, 1985—-Juvenile literature. | African American basketball players—Biography—Juvenile literature. | Basketball players—United States—Biography—Juvenile literature.
Classification: LCC GV884.P376 F57 2020 (print) | LCC GV884.P376 (ebook) | DDC 796.323092 [B]—dc23
LC record available at https://lccn.loc.gov/2019028770
LC ebook record available at https://lccn.loc.gov/2019028771

Manufactured in the United States of America
1-46752-47743-9/16/2019

CONTENTS

TAKING CARE
OF BUSINESS

Chris Paul celebrates making a three-pointer.

Spinning spotlights lit up the basketball court as music filled the arena. Fans wearing dark red Houston Rockets gear settled into their seats to cheer on the home team.

- **Date of birth:** May 6, 1985

- **Position: point guard**

- **League:** National Basketball Association (NBA)

- **Professional highlights:** won the 2005–2006 Rookie of the Year award; led the NBA in **steals** five times; voted to play in nine All-Star Games

- **Personal highlights:** grew up in Lewisville, North Carolina; started the Chris Paul Family Foundation in 2005; loves to bowl

Paul drives past Utah's defense for a basket.

A referee threw the ball into the air for the game's opening **tip-off**. It was time to play!

Chris Paul and the Rockets were playing against the Utah Jazz in the first round of the 2019 National Basketball Association (NBA) playoffs. Houston led the series 3–1. If they could win this game, they would win the series and advance to the next round.

The Rockets won the tip-off. Paul received a pass and dribbled in a curving path toward the basket. The Utah defender trying to stop him couldn't keep up. Suddenly, 13 feet (4 m) from the basket, Paul stopped and shot the ball. It sailed through the hoop for the first two points of the game.

As a point guard, Paul's main job is to run his team's offense. He makes sure all offensive players are doing what they're supposed to do on every play. He passes the ball to teammates for open shots, and he scores when others are covered.

Paul works hard on defense too. When Utah missed their first shot, he grabbed the **rebound**. Later in the first quarter, he snatched a Utah pass for his first steal of the game. Paul has the most steals of all active NBA players.

Houston had a six-point lead at the start of the fourth quarter, but Utah fought back. With less than eight minutes to play, the game was tied 80–80. Then Paul made another 13-foot (4 m) shot. After the Rockets stopped the Jazz from scoring, Paul sank a long three-point basket to put his team ahead by five. Houston led the rest of the way and won the game 100–93.

Paul had 15 points, eight rebounds, and three steals in the win. He was thrilled to beat Utah and advance in the **playoffs**. "We wanted to take care of business tonight," he said. "It's always hard to beat a team and close them out."

Paul (*left*) poses with his parents and brother.

Chris Paul was born on May 6, 1985.

His brother, C. J., is about two years older than he is. They lived with their parents, Robin Jones and Charles Paul, in Lewisville, North Carolina.

When Chris was three, his father built a basketball court for the boys in the basement. He marked the court with tape and set up two plastic toy hoops. The brothers loved to compete against each other. Chris was smaller, but he never backed down from his older brother.

Paul playing in a celebrity football game

Chris liked football too. He played defense and quarterback on **Pop Warner** teams. He was so good that he played on West Forsyth High School's **varsity** team as a freshman. But in basketball, he was stuck on the junior varsity team.

Chris's nickname, CP3, comes from his family. He shares initials with his father and older brother. His father is CP1, C. J. is CP2, and Chris is CP3.

Being tall is a major advantage in basketball. Tall people can reach high for rebounds and stretch their long arms to block shots. As a freshman in 2000, Chris stood only 5 feet (1.5 m) tall. Basketball coaches didn't think he was tall enough for the varsity team.

Chris played junior varsity basketball for two years. He grew, improved, and moved up to varsity his junior year. But November of his senior year,

Paul dribbles and looks for open teammates at Wake Forest.

tragedy struck the Paul family. Nathaniel Jones, Chris's grandfather, was killed outside his home.

Chris had been especially close to Jones. For two days after his grandfather's death, Chris felt sick. Then he played a game for Forsyth and scored 61 points. He missed a **free throw** on purpose and left the game. He had scored one point in honor of each year of his grandfather's life.

Paul made 86 percent of his free throws in the 2018–2019 season.

By his senior season, Chris stood 6 feet (1.8 m) tall. He averaged 30.8 points, 6 steals, and 5.9 rebounds per game for Forsyth. The team lost just three games all season.

Paul smiles at a press conference after being drafted by the Hornets.

After high school, Paul attended Wake Forest University in Winston-Salem, North Carolina. In the 2003–2004 season, he set Wake Forest freshman records for steals, **assists**, and other stats. He played just as well as a sophomore.

In 2005, Paul entered the NBA Draft. It was held in New York City on June 28. He didn't have to wait long to be chosen. The New Orleans Hornets took him with the fourth overall pick.

STAYING STRONG

Paul has to work harder than other players because of his height.

Paul has never been the tallest player on his team. His success is due to his skill and a lot of hard work. It all began with his father and brother.

Paul's father taught him how to dribble with his left hand.

When Chris and C. J. were young, their father played basketball at a nearby gym. He often brought the boys with him. But they weren't there just to watch. He had the brothers dribble with their right arms behind their backs. This helped them get used to dribbling with their left arms. He also covered their eyes to teach them to dribble without looking at the ball.

Paul fuels his workouts with healthful food. But sometimes he can't resist delicious snacks that aren't as good for him. "It's French fries—that's my favorite that I just can't say no to," Paul said.

As an NBA player, Paul continues to sharpen his skills. He learns plays and does shooting **drills** with his teammates. But with 82 games on the schedule, most teams don't have many practice sessions during the season. The players need to rest on their days off.

Paul practices a slam dunk during shootaround.

Paul and his teammates work on their skills before games during **shootaround**. At shootaround, coaches talk to the team about that night's opponent. They go over new plays and discuss the other team's

Before exercises, Paul relaxes in a steam room to get his mind and body ready.

favorite plays. Then the players shoot and run drills on the court.

After the NBA season, Paul doesn't sit around. He works out all year. "When you're young . . . you can get out of shape and then you just get right back," he said. "When you get older, you have to work at it." He often starts the day in a steam room. The hot, steam-filled space helps him relax. It's too wet for most phones and other devices, so it's a good place for Paul to think without distractions.

After the steam room, Paul exercises. He does drills standing on a ball that wobbles and forces him to work to stay on top. This improves his strength and balance and makes his ankles and other joints tougher to prevent injuries. Paul also likes to do chin-ups to strengthen his upper body.

As Paul has gotten older, he has done more stretching exercises. He stretches his muscles every night before bed. He uses a foam roller—a rolled-up pad. Stretching with a foam roller helps Paul recover from workouts and feel better in the morning.

Paul stretches before games to prevent his muscles from tightening.

Paul played for the Los Angeles Clippers from 2011 to 2016.

Paul and his foundation host a holiday shopping event for kids.

Playing basketball has made Paul incredibly rich. After the 2018–2019 season, he had earned about $200 million in the NBA. Then the Rockets signed him to a new contract worth more than $159 million. He uses some of his money to help other people.

In 2005, Paul and his family started the CP3 Foundation. After his family became more involved, the name changed to the Chris Paul Family Foundation. The group helps people in North Carolina and around the country. They work to make sure everyone has access to education and sports. They build places for kids to play and help students pay for school. In 2016, ESPN gave Paul a special award for his work with the group.

Paul visits kids in his foundation's after-school program.

Paul loves music, and he says he can't live without it. "I listen to music all day, every day," he said. "We have a speaker system in the bathroom."

Paul likes different styles of music, and he listens to a lot of rap. He's friends with rap megastar Jay-Z. But Paul has also been influenced by his son, Chris Jr., who loves Justin Bieber. Little Chris, as Paul calls his son, even got to sit with Bieber at one of his dad's games.

Chris Jr. and Justin Bieber watching one of Paul's games

Paul celebrates the launch of his sneakers that have a chevron symbol for his grandfather.

The family started the foundation in honor of Nathaniel Jones. Paul has never forgotten his grandfather. He still has the basketball that he used to score 61 points to honor Jones.

Paul's shoe designs also honor his grandfather. NBA superstars often help design their own shoes. Paul always includes a symbol in his shoe designs that was important to Jones.

Basketball isn't Paul's only sports passion. He loves bowling, and he even owns a team in the Professional Bowlers Association. The team, L.A.X., has five players that compete in bowling events around the world.

Paul uses his love of bowling to raise money for his foundation. In 2018, he held a celebrity bowling event in Texas. Paul and a teammate beat baseball superstar and professional bowler Mookie Betts's team in the championship.

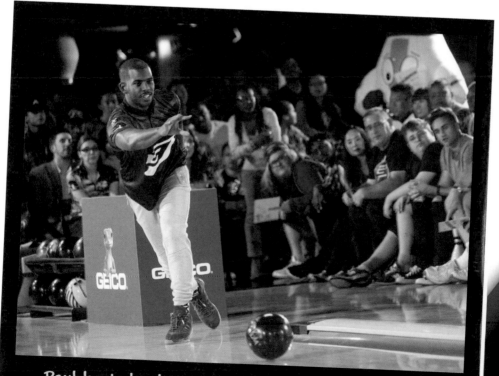

Paul hosts bowling tournaments for his foundation.

Paul rushes past Stephen Curry during the 2019 playoffs.

Chris Paul has years of pro basketball ahead of him, yet he's already had a great career. He became a star right away, winning the NBA Rookie of the Year award in 2005–2006. Since then, he has proven to be one of the game's best year after year.

Paul shoots a three-pointer against Golden State.

Paul led the NBA in steals in five different seasons. He had the most assists in the league three times and ranks seventh on the NBA's all-time career assists list. He's been voted to play in nine All-Star Games.

The Hornets traded Paul to the Los Angeles Clippers in 2011. In 2017, the Clippers traded him to the Rockets. In return for Paul, the Clippers received seven players, a draft pick, and more than $600,000 from Houston.

Paul greets fans before facing the Jazz in 2019.

Paul's personal stats are amazing, but his teams have had less success. In 2018, his team made it to the playoff semifinals for the first time. The Rockets lost to the Golden State Warriors in seven games. After beating the Jazz in the 2019 playoffs, Houston faced Golden State again. This time the Warriors won in six games.

Paul will keep pushing himself and his teammates in the years to come. He wants to be the NBA champion more than ever. "We have one goal here, and that's to win," he said.

Paul hopes to win the championship with his team.

No current NBA player has more steals than Paul. On the NBA's all-time steals list, he ranks alongside some of the most legendary players in league history. Where do you think he'll rank when he retires?

Most Career Steals in NBA History

Player	Steals
John Stockton	3,265
Jason Kidd	2,684
Michael Jordan	2,514
Gary Payton	2,445
Maurice Cheeks	2,310
Scottie Pippen	2,307
Clyde Drexler	2,207
Hakeem Olajuwon	2,162
Chris Paul	**2,122**
Alvin Robertson	2,112

Source Notes

7 "Harden Helps Rockets Eliminate Jazz with 100–93 Win," *ESPN*, April 24, 2019, http://www.espn.com /nba/recap?gameId=401126861.

15 Matthew Jussim, "NBA Star Chris Paul's Key Training Method for Staying Strong, and How the Rockets Can Challenge the Warriors," *Men's Journal*, accessed June 1, 2019, https://www.mensjournal .com/health-fitness/nba-star-chris-pauls-key-training -method-staying-strong-and-how-rockets-can/.

16 Jussim.

21 Clay Skipper, "The Three Things Chris Paul Has to Do on Game Day," *GQ*, October 30, 2018, https:// www.gq.com/story/chris-paul-daily-routine.

27 Alysha Tsuji, "Chris Paul quoted 'Talladega Nights' While Talking about Rockets' Goal of Winning a Title," *USA Today*, July 14, 2017, https://ftw.usatoday .com/2017/07/chris-paul-rockets-championship-ricky -bobby-talladega-nights-quote-win-first-last.

Glossary

assists: passes that lead to scores

drills: exercises designed to improve skills

free throw: an uncontested shot from behind the free throw line that is sometimes awarded when the other team commits a foul

playoffs: series of games played to decide a champion

point guard: the player in charge of a team's offense

Pop Warner: a group that organizes youth football leagues and other activities

rebound: the act of grabbing and controlling the ball after a missed shot

shootaround: a time before a basketball game when players warm up and practice on the court

steals: taking possession of the ball from the other team

tip-off: the act of throwing the basketball into the air to begin play

varsity: the top team at a school

Further Information

Chris Paul Family Foundation
https://chrispaul3.com/foundation/

Fishman, Jon M. *Mookie Betts*. Minneapolis: Lerner Publications, 2020.

Houston Rockets
https://www.nba.com/rockets/

Jr. NBA
https://jr.nba.com/

Monson, James. *Behind the Scenes Basketball*. Minneapolis: Lerner Publications, 2020.

Schaller, Bob. *The Everything Kids' Basketball Book: The All-Time Greats, Legendary Teams, Today's Superstars—and Tips on Playing like a Pro*. 3rd ed. New York: Adams Media, 2017.

Index

Photo Acknowledgments

Image credits: Tim Warner/Getty Images, pp. 4, 13, 24–26; Bob Levey/Getty Images, p. 6; Kelly Kline/Getty Images, pp. 8, 22; Allen Berezovsky/Getty Images, p. 9; Bob Leverone/Sporting News Archive/Getty Images, p. 10; Stacy Revere/Getty Images, p. 11; AP Photo/Bill Haber, p. 12; Andy Lyons/Getty Images, p. 14; Ezra Shaw/Getty Images, p. 15; miljko/Getty Images, p. 16; Sean Gardner/Getty Images, p. 17; Sean M. Haffey/Getty Images, p. 18; Jerod Harris/Getty Images, p. 19; Erika Goldring/Stringer/Getty Images, p. 20; AP Photo/Charles Baus, p. 21; Imeh Akpanudosen/Stringer/Getty Images, p. 23; Quinn Harris/Getty Images, p. 27.

Cover: Stacy Revere/Getty Images.